Contents

IF THE DRAGON WINS
BUILD ANOTHER CASTLE

The ABC's of Grief

M. KATHARYN MEYERS

M. Katharyn Meyers

Published by
Sugarloaf Publishers
P.O. Box 3833
Littleton, CO 80161-3833

Cover photograph by
Michael P. Meyers

Cover design and book layout by
Emelene Russell Advertising & Design
Daniel Pahang, Art Director

Manufactured in the United States of America

April 1998

10 9 8 7 6 5 4 3 2 1

Library of Congress Catalog Card Number 98-90233

ISBN – 0-9663564-0-3

For Mike

Acknowledgments

It takes a long time to write a book, even a little one like this. And it takes a lot of help. Help from family, friends, neighbors, and one particular editor at Paulist Press.

To my older son Mike who was there for me even when I wasn't or couldn't be a very good parent, thank you. I'm proud of you.

SINCERE GRATITUDE GOES TO:
Rob Baldwin, my neighbor, who read an early manuscript and made valuable editing suggestions.
My parents, Pete and Bernice Meyers.
My sisters, Patti Klingensmith and Rosalie Buckley and their families in Wyoming.
Maria Maggi at the Paulist Press. Maria read my manuscript, made an offer and made me believe that there was something to this little book.
Emelene Russell and Daniel Pahang of Emelene Russell Advertising & Design who produced such a beautiful book and provided expert advise about the creation of the volume.

There are others who made grieving and
the process of moving on bearable.
Special thanks go to:
Roger Radomsky, Laramie County Coroner, whose
kindness and very special advice, I will never forget.
The Thursday group; Dorothy Elder, Dorothy Rome,
Dorothy Olds, Sunni Patton, Phyllis Hoover, and
Marjorie Carroll who provided spiritual help and
wonderful friendship for which I will always
be grateful.
Jessie Valas who was instrumental in the
healing process.
Patti Jo Patterson who prayed "all the time."
Compassionate Friends, the Denver Chapter.
Kay Nichols, Dorothy Kircher, Carol Obenchain,
Jerry Bennett, Dennis Brosius, Elizabeth Reisa,
Charlene and Jim Lewis, Bonnie and Dexter
Wedemeyer and their family, and Darrell Pendley, Ph.D.
All are friends of the highest order.

I will be forever indebted to:
Carol Renne who supports me 100%.
Julia Adams who saved my life and doesn't know it.
Tony Adams and his fabulous cookies.

Introduction

In 1986 both my younger son Chris and one of my brothers, Jack, died. Jack died March 22, 1986. Chris became ill in June and died November 26, 1986, the day before Thanksgiving. Suddenly I had forgotten what deep pain and sorrow were even though my mother died after a long illness when I was 25, and when I was 10, my brothers, sisters and I were placed in The Wyoming State Children's Home. These were great losses and I know I grieved and developed some coping mechanisms but it wasn't until after the loss of my son and brother that I learned about the process called bereavement.

That's how this little book came about. Out of my deep need for healing, I began to seek information about grieving. I thought I was going crazy but found out that things that were happening to me were "normal" for people who suffered such overwhelming loss. It gave me great comfort to know that I wasn't going crazy and it gave me hope.

Every day we experience loss. Every day we go through minor transitions which seem natural to us. We lose a day and get a bit older. If we had a disagreement with someone who is important to us, a family member or coworker, we hopefully processed the event. If there was upsetting news during the day, we adjusted. During our lifetime and in the course of the shifts of our regular day, we have developed coping mechanisms and see this as part of life's inevitability.

It's when we experience a major event that we think something strange and foreign has happened. It may be the loss of a beloved family member; child, partner, or pet. Or it could be the separation from the work we perform. It might be a sudden illness, an accident or theft. Or an earthquake, tornado, hurricane or fire. Perhaps it's the loss of a limb, bodily function, or we're threatened with some debilitating and/or life threatening disease. When a major loss occurs, we have been separated from an important structure in our lives, not just a minor circumstance.

The grieving process begins the minute we experience a sense of separation from someone or something we regarded as valuable and necessary in our lives. A pet provided companionship and unconditional love. If it was a partner, a source of livelihood and stability may be gone and if it was a child, the most precious gift in the world has been taken from you.

It's at this time that we forget that we have coping mechanisms or the ones we have developed don't seem to be working. The more emotionally invested we are in the relationship the more profound the grief.

We wonder where our minds went. To another planet yet to be named? Concentration is difficult and we might be very emotional. We want to know why this happened. I don't know why these things happen. All I know is that they do and that there is a process that we go through to make the transition. Becoming aware of this process will help you through the difficult times.

The process is natural, healthy, and necessary to protect our mental, physical, and emotional well being.

This book provides information about the grief process and suggests ways in which you can cope and take care of yourself as you work through your grief.

Grief has four stages as defined by the Grief Education Institute of Denver, Colorado. We cycle through these four stages during the mourning period. They aren't hard and fast stages. We tend to move back and forth between them depending on where we are in the recovery process.

The first stage is SHOCK. We're dazed, in a state of disbelief. It's unreal. Our balance has been tampered with. The second stage is PROTEST. We're searching and yearning, trying to make some sense of what has happened. We wonder how this could have happened.

In the third stage, DISORGANIZATION, we realize our lives have been turned upside down. We have to experience things again for the first time without our loved one or the something that was part of our lives. Nothing seems to fit like it used to. Life is a puzzle and we're trying to put the pieces together but pieces are missing. It's during this phase that we begin making a different puzzle, one without whatever it is that's gone.

REORGANIZATION is the final stage and the ongoing stage in our lives. We're continually rearranging our lives, learning new skills, meeting new people, making new friends, deepening existing relationships or letting old patterns go. We are growing, changing, and learning to live with what life presents to us as we walk through our daily lives.

Becoming aware of this process led me to understand what was happening to me. Participating in a Compassionate Friends support group, a group for parents who have lost children, let me see that other people were experiencing some of the same symptoms I was.

As part of my healing, I developed a workshop called "The Cycles of Change," which helps others to understand the process of grieving. Some of my research into the grieving process for my workshops has been put together in this book and was used to support my degree in psychology.

It is my hope that the ABC format will provide a trigger for you to remember some of what will be happening to you during your life changing events. I hope these are tools that will help you grow and not get stuck in the process and that it will be of help to you as you move through the difficult changes brought about by the losses life will inevitably present to us.

We used to have a drawing on our refrigerator with the caption, "Sometimes the Dragon Wins." Come along with me and learn to "Build Another Castle."

Good grief to you all.

An important part of the process is ACCEPTING the reality of the loss. If your loss is very recent, within a few months, you might not read any further because that's not something you want to hear. However, at some point, accepting the reality of the loss will help you move through the cycles of change that are inevitable in life's process.

As we accept the reality, we begin to ADJUST to an environment without whatever it is that no longer supports us: The loved one, the work, the pet, the limb, our sight. The list is endless. At this point, you might think about what loss(es) you have experienced.

If it's helpful, make a list. Making a list will help you become aware of the changes happening in your life. Then ask yourself what you're doing to adjust in this situation? Don't worry if nothing comes to mind. As you continue reading, make notes about what you can do to move through this period of change.

A

ACCEPTING
ADJUST

β

BEREAVED
BURYING

When we feel the loss of people or things around us, we are BEREAVED and we mourn. To be bereaved means to lose something or someone precious. To mourn is to be burdened by sorrow. When we express the sorrow, we show signs that we are adapting to the loss.

Sometimes we try to behave as if nothing is wrong and when we do this our physical and mental health suffer. Loss is real and BURYING your feelings will only prolong your healing and may damage your health.

CRY. Crying releases pressure and stress. IT's
OKAY TO CRY.

When we cry we need to drink lots of water
because the electrolyte balances within our
bodies get out of whack. Sometimes our sense
of thirst gets overridden during this time, so
it is good to make a conscious effort to drink
2 quarts of water each day.

Signs that you may not have enough water
are tightness in the throat, diminished
appetite, or a thick tongue. Avoiding
alcohol, drugs, and caffeine will also help
because they tend to dehydrate.

CHANGING your environment too quickly
after a loss is not wise because we need
the stability of familiar surroundings.
Give yourself time to adjust before making
major changes.

D

You know you're in DANGER when:
- Your mourning turns into long term depression.
- You have persistent thoughts of not wanting to live anymore.
- You turn to substance abuse to solve your anguish.
- You don't take care of yourself by eating right, exercising, staying in touch with people who love and care for you, and getting plenty of rest.

DEPRESSION and thoughts of suicide are fairly common. When it begins to get in the way of your productivity and prevents you from taking care of yourself physically, mentally or emotionally, it's a sign that you're in trouble.

SEEK HELP IMMEDIATELY! There are many wonderful therapists and doctors who can help you. Before you go for long term counseling, ask to interview the therapist to see if there's a match between the two of you. Call a support group and ask for references. Don't settle for just anybody. Check the person out. Reputable professionals will gladly grant you an interview and even help in the process of selecting the right treatment for you.

E

EXERCISE
ENERGY

EXERCISE will help keep you not only fit but sane. Physical exercise every day will help you keep regular sleep patterns which might be erratic for a while. It will help control your appetite whether you tend to overeat or undereat. And the most important of all, it will handle your depression. Studies show that aerobic exercise on a daily basis prevents depression. It works better than antidepressants. Exercise provides ENERGY and erases the chemicals which build up on the brain cells and cause depression.

Walking is the best exercise. It's the easiest to do and the least harmful to your body. Thirty-five minutes a day or one hour, three to four times a week will help keep you fit, mentally and physically. Before you begin a program, if you're not already in one, check with your doctor to see what's best for your circumstances.

During this time it will be natural to have FEELINGS of anger, rage, sadness, despair, frustration and many others. All feelings are natural and needed. Feelings help us to process the loss. Negative feelings such as anger have gotten a lot of bad press, not because they are bad, but because they are used in a negative way. Positive feelings of anger stir in us positive needs to make a change, to make a difference.

It's okay to express all of your feelings. Let them out, let them go. Make friends with them by acknowledging that they are part of you.

FORGIVENESS is the way to let go. Forgiveness means "to give up FEELINGS of anger, hatred, or resentment." It literally means to let go of the feelings that keep us blocked. It has nothing to do with letting the other person(s) or events off the hook. They will always be responsible for what they did.

But we cannot be free if we hold onto negative feelings and attitudes that keep us from living fully.

Ask yourself, "What are these resentments costing me?" When you determine how they have limited your life in the areas of spirituality, relationships, career, family, and others, you'll be eager to let them go.

To GRIEVE means "to remember." During the process of grieving we remember over and over again so that our memories become fixed in our minds forever. Our memories are often all we have and it's important to get the story fixed in our minds. It's the greatest GIFT we can give ourselves.

Setting GOALS will help you see a future even if you can't believe in one yet. Make a list of things you haven't accomplished yet. Use the following areas: Spirituality, Family, Relationships, Career, Home, Physical, Sexuality, Personality. Determine one thing that you will do in three of these areas that will move you towards accomplishing a goal and Do It Now!

A simple but necessary goal in the area of physical well being might be to get up in the morning and go to bed in the evening at the same time as you're used to. Keeping to regular patterns, as much as you can, will help you recover faster. This might seem rather silly, but it's important.

G

GRIEVE
GIFT
GOALS

H

HUGS
HEALING
HAPPINESS

HUGS are necessary for HEALING and growth. Just as babies die from marasmus, the lack of touching, we wither and sometimes die when we don't experience touching. If you're not being touched by people close to you, try a weekly massage. It is healing in itself.

Teddy bears are a great source of hugs and nurturing, just ask any five year old. I knew a therapist who carried her teddy bear in a car seat in her car. One of my bears is a big black cuddly bear named Bart. When nothing else works, Bart is there. He doesn't talk back. He never says no. He's always there just eager and waiting to provide me with a hug.

HAPPINESS will return. Expect it!

INSECURITY is a common feeling because something that was supporting us is no longer within our realm of experience. Sometimes this makes us overly dependent on others. There's nothing wrong with being a little dependent. It can make others feel needed and wanted. However, when it becomes a burden, we need to take a look at ourselves and see what can be done differently.

INVESTING in new relationships and/or developing new or reestablishing previous INTERESTS will help move you past this phase. Feelings of insecurity will be replaced by feelings of self confidence and self worth when something new is learned or a new relationship blossoms.

9

INSECURITY
INVEST
INTERESTS

J

JOURNALING
JOIN
JUNK

JOURNALING is a terrific way to measure your progress. People who keep diaries are often surprised by what they thought and felt when they review older entries. It is also a safe place to write out and express your deepest feelings and concerns.

JOIN a support group. It is a safe atmosphere in which to relive your memories, solve problems, hear other viewpoints, and get hugs. Your local newspaper usually will have a list of groups.

JUNK food is so tempting now because it is so comforting. Do your best to avoid it. If you can't resist, really enjoy!

Expect and appreciate KINDNESS. You deserve to be loved and nurtured during this time. Let people take care of you through their kind acts.

Your mind will want to trick you now by telling you things like, "It's all your fault. You're a bad person if this happened to you." Don't believe it. KICK those thoughts right out of your mind. Picture yourself giving them the boot. Go ahead. Yell at them. "OUT, NO, FALSE." Do, something, anything that will stop the negative self-talk.

Be a KID again. Learn to play. Make a list of ways in which you like to play. My list includes and is not limited to: chew bubble gum, fly a kite, play jacks, marbles, build a sand castle, blow bubbles, make something, skip rope, ride a bike (wear a helmet), sing, dance. The list is endless. You can come up with your own list. Hang it up where you can see it and then commit to playing once a week for a couple of hours.

KINDNESS
KICK
KID

L

LONGING
LAUGH
LOVE

It will be natural to experience some LONGING after your loss. You may feel the presence of something or someone who is gone. Some events may trigger intense emotions and memories. These are natural feelings and you're not weird or crazy for having them. These will usually happen within a few months after the loss when emotions are new and intense. Try to see these as part of the process of placing memories into permanent storage.

Some people think they aren't entitled to LAUGH or LOVE anymore. But laughter helps us heal. It stimulates the life in our bodies and minds and coaxes them towards health. Love will return. Although you think it won't, love will again be part of your life and YES, you will love and be loved again.

Make a list of things you love to do. What's on your goal list? Are there activities you love? Doing what we love nurtures our spirits and promotes healthy minds and bodies.

Create as many MEMORIES as you can. Make a scrapbook, write stories, put together a picture album, or plant a tree in memory. The better you fix the loved one in your memory the better your healing.

One of the ways we remember is to talk about our loss. Talk, Talk, Talk. Tell anyone who will listen. People who wish you would shut up don't understand that you're just fixing the memories in your mind.

MEDITATE, use progressive relaxation or biofeedback to relax during the day. These practices have been shown to give you a deeper rest than sleep. There are many good books about meditation. Two of my favorites are, *The Art of Meditation* by Joel Goldsmith and *Meditation, An Eight Point Program* by Ecknath Eswaran. Eswaran's book provides a step by step guide and the Goldsmith book is spiritually based.

M

MEMORIES
MEDITATE

Many local bookstores have audiotapes that will help you learn to relax the body from head to toe which is what progressive relaxation accomplishes.

Biofeedback is usually learned in a clinical setting, however, Barbara Brown wrote a great book entitled, *Stress and The Art of Biofeedback,* in which she describes the biofeedback process.

NURTURE yourself. We all need a nurturing social network. Make a list of the people upon whom you can depend. Call them when you need to talk. Let people know what you need so they can support you.

Watch what you eat. It's easy to let our NUTRITIONAL needs slide. We might not have an appetite or eating may be a way to hide feelings. Eating well-balanced meals will keep your body and mind functioning at their optimum. Include plenty of fresh fruits and vegetables plus whole grains and a moderate amount of protein. Love your body and mind by taking care of them with good, nutritional food and drink.

N

NURTURE
NUTRITION

O

ORDER your days. If your life isn't or hasn't been orderly, establish a routine. Life is all jumbled up right now and putting order in your days, weeks, and months will help you manage an already turbulent time.

ORDER
ORGANIZED

When loss occurs, our lives become disORGANIZED. During the grieving process we will be reORGANIZING our lives and setting new priorities and goals. These new priorities will be promoting our adjustment to a different life, a life without whatever it is we lost. A life that may include more compassion and consideration for those who will experience losses in their lives.

The kindest and most wonderful people are those who have survived great loss and understand the need to be cared for in a compassionate and loving way.

We are not being PUNISHED by God. No matter what you think, remove this from your thought process. God loves us and would not inflict this kind of pain on us.

Guilt feelings are the sickness of the world. They are poison and keep us from forgiving ourselves and each other. We may have done something to hurt another person but their absence has not happened to punish us. If we are being punished, it is because we choose to punish ourselves. God does not want this. "You are His beloved child, in whom He is well pleased." Our souls grieve when we are hurting ourselves physically or mentally.

PRAYER is the key. Not the begging, beseeching kind but the kind Jim Lewis, a wonderful minister I knew, used to talk about. He said, "Sit down, shut up and listen." Listen in the quiet. I know that listening is hard to do and even harder when

ρ

PUNISHED
PRAYER

your mind is full of grief thoughts. You need to be quiet. In the quiet you will learn to slow down, to ask and even to receive the answer to your prayer.

Spend five minutes a day in quiet contemplation. Start with one minute or 30 seconds if a minute is too long. Gradually increase the time to five minutes. Ask for healing. Be quiet and listen. Be still and be peaceful. Be healed.

Some people move through the loss process QUICKLY. Others take a long time. The important thing to remember is that, IT TAKES AS LONG AS IT TAKES. Don't beat yourself up if in a few months you're not "back to normal."

Sometimes family members, employers, and friends don't understand what you're going through. Help them by providing information such as this book so they know that, IT TAKES AS LONG AS IT TAKES. They'll be grateful you did when it comes their turn to go through a loss.

Sometimes friends and even family may choose to move out of your life. I often hear from parents who have lost children or partners and spouses who are widowed or divorcing, that certain "friends" no longer call them or have excluded them from their circle.

2

QUICKLY

I call this "AITS," the Ain't In Touch Syndrome. AITS people are so afraid of catching what you have that they just seem to drop out of your life. They are afraid that this is a deadly disease and they don't want to catch it so they disappear. If they do stay in your life, they may have little compassion or patience. They have no idea the hurt they cause.

My advice to this person is for them to join a loss support group and try to learn about and "feel" what we are going through. Because, when it comes their turn, they're in for big time shock and trouble.

Sometimes we become the ones who drop out of other people's lives. Be careful that you aren't the AITS person. Stay in touch with those who have supported you in the past.

During the fourth stage of loss, we enter the phase of Reorganization. We have adjusted to the loss. We have established new routines, made new friends, if that is what the situation called for, and our lives are even better than they were before the loss occurred. This is because we have developed new coping mechanisms and strengthened our old ones.

At some point expect to experience a feeling of Release, a letting go of the pain associated with your loss. You'll experience reentering life with new perspectives and insights. You might even be willing to forgive some of the "AITS" people that dropped out of your life and want to return now that they see you have recovered from your disease.

R

Reorganization
Release

S

Survivor
Survive

You are a Survivor. You have weathered the storm. You've fought the battle and won. If the dragon won, you've built another castle or are in the process of building one. You've discovered that different losses are not a contest. The death of my son is not greater than the death of your pet. The loss of one person's home that is destroyed by fire is not greater than the other's whose partner suddenly died. Cancer is not "better than" a lost limb. And someone who loses their wallet can be just as devastated as I was.

Those of us who have experienced great personal tragedy know that the process of grief includes great personal suffering and we appreciate the work necessary to Survive. We become the healers of the world through our understanding and compassion.

Take TIME for yourself, lots of it. You're worth it. Spend time doing things you love to do. These are the things that will restore wholeness.

TAKING CARE OF OURSELVES means:
- Eating a well balanced diet
- Getting plenty of rest including relaxation exercises
- Doing forgiveness exercises daily
- Doing what we love
- Making play a part of our lives, being a kid again
- Drinking plenty of water
- Having a nurturing social network

7

TIME
TAKING CARE
OF OURSELVES

U

UTILIZE
UNDERSTAND

UTILIZE community resources. Many churches have loss support groups or provide workshops and seminars. Lots of people are going through loss and they need and want to be supported just like you.

UNDERSTAND that this is a period of transition, an ending and a beginning. There's a process to it. You can do it and YOU'RE WORTH IT.

One day you will feel VICTORIOUS! You will have built your new castle and the dragon will have been slain. You will have pleasant memories, and there will be joy in your heart. You have done your work, processed your feelings, and have a plan for your future.

You have your mind back. You still don't know where it was, but you're happy it's back.

V

VICTORIOUS

W

WALKED
WILL
WONDER

Congratulations, you have WALKED the path of loss and endured. Your WILL is strong again and now you are settled in your strength, knowing that nothing can disturb your peace. Sure there will be disappointments, loss, and heartbreak again, but you have developed new and strengthened old coping mechanisms. You are triumphant and ready to take on the world.

You are a WONDER.

Put an X on the day in your life when you feel your new self emerge. There will be many X's on many days as you'll discover. Think about how wonderful it would be if you had an X on every day from now on because every day you felt a revelation within yourself about the wonder that you are.

X

X the Day

Y

You

You are an important and valuable person.
You are remarkable.
You are unique.
You are creative.
You are love.
You are loved.
You are.
You.

Develop a ZEAL and ZEST for life. Here is an affirmation, which might be helpful, "I have ZEAL, ZEST and enthusiasm for life and this ZEAL, ZEST and enthusiasm support me in all that I do."

Perhaps you'd like to use this affirmation every morning. Stand in front of the mirror and look into your beautiful eyes and say to yourself the above affirmation and then add, "I AM WONDERFUL."

And, so it is!

3

ZEAL
ZEST

Conclusion

It is my wish that you find comfort in these few pages and that they provide you with hope. I find comfort in memories, the memories of Chris and Jack and the new ones I've created since their departures. I remember them both with great love, caring and happy memories.

I remember playing Scrabble with my brother Jack. He nearly always won. One of his pastimes was to read the Encyclopedia Britannica. I remember his stories about the bald eagles on Casper Mountain in Wyoming. He seemed to have a personal relationship with them. And, I remember how much he loved his family.

When I remember my son Chris, I remember how much fun he was, what a marvelous sense of humor he had. I remember standing in a long line at the drug store dressed in my finest and he wanted me to get something trivial. I had $20.00 in my wallet and remarked that this was it until payday. He said in a loud voice, "Well, haven't we got our welfare check yet?" I was stunned and he had this twinkle in his eye, saying "gotcha!" We both started to laugh and so did everyone in the line.

When he became ill, he remembered what it was like to be well, to be a talented artist. He missed being whole, being able to laugh at the movies, being silly and having a good time. His brother Mike and I missed it, too. We missed a bright, energetic, fun-loving guy. What I remember most, however, was his love of people and of me. I miss that most of all.

I think of them both with the fondest of memories. I know that God blesses them both on their journeys and continues to take care of those of us who make our way on this life's journey.

May you find blessings, happiness, and peace on your journey.

Kathy